Mother's Day
5/12/1974

Laura & Tina
Mulston

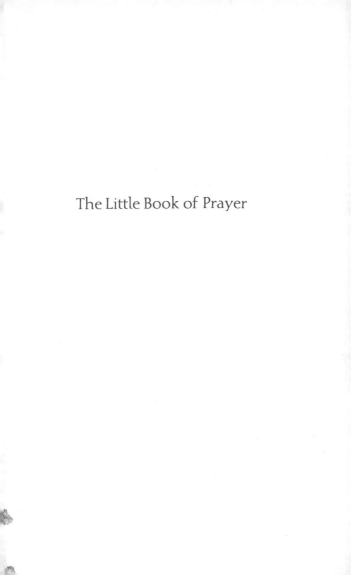

The Little Book of Prayer

The Little Book Of Prayer

With Inspiration From the Psalms

Selected and Written
By Gail Harano Cunningham

Illustrated by Linda Welty

Hallmark Editions

I lift up my eyes to the hills.
  From whence does my help come?
  My help comes from the Lord,
  who made heaven and earth.

Psalm 121:1-2

I need you, Lord.
Because of you I find meaning
and joy in the world.

*I will sing to the Lord, because
he has dealt bountifully with me.*

Psalm 13:6

Thank you for today, Lord,
and all its possibilities.
Help me to show my love
as I use the special gift
you've given me.

I will bless the Lord at all times.

Psalm 34:1

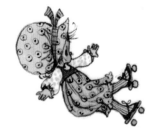

Dear Lord, help me to turn
my helplessness into strength,
my frustration into patience,
my anger into love.

The Lord is my shepherd,
I shall not want.

                    Psalm 23:1

Lord, help me
not to be anxious
about the future,
to remember that
you are always there
knowing my needs
before I realize them myself.

Make me to know thy ways, O Lord;
teach me thy paths.

Psalm 25:4

There's so much to learn, Lord.
Help me, as I learn,
to always remember
that obedience to you
is the beginning of wisdom.

The Lord is good to all,
and his compassion
is over all that he has made.

Psalm 145:9

Help me
to be a good neighbor, Lord,
to do my part
in making the world
gentler, kinder, better.

When the cares of my heart are many,
thy consolations cheer my soul.

Psalm 94:19

There is no day so dark
that the gifts of sunshine,
love, and friendly laughter
cannot brighten it.
Thank you for these gifts.

O Lord, how manifold are thy works!
  In wisdom hast thou made them all;
  the earth is full of thy creatures.

                                    Psalm 104:24

Dear Lord,
we are amazed and humble
when we think of your creation
and awed by the responsibility
you have given us.

Behold, how good and pleasant it is
when brothers dwell in unity!

Psalm 133:1

Lord, we thank you for each other…
for the good times we have shared,
for the kinship we know
as your children.

Bless the Lord, O my soul,
and forget not all his benefits.

Psalm 103:2

Lord, help me
to search for answers
and to see my problems
as opportunities.

O give thanks to the Lord,
  for he is good;
    his steadfast love endures for ever!

Psalm 118:1

Among the hurry and worry
and change in our lives,
Lord, only your love is constant.
Thank you, Lord,
for always being there.

The Lord is near to all
who call upon him,
to all who call upon him in truth.

Psalm 145:18

Lord, please be with those I love
who are far away.
Though I cannot comfort them,
laugh with them, share with them,
I know that you can do all things
and love them as I do.

I love the Lord,
   because he has heard my voice
   and my supplications.
   Because he inclined his ear to me,
   therefore I will call on him
   as long as I live.

   Psalm 116:1-2

Thank you, Lord,
for providing more than I need,
for helping me grow.

Unless the Lord builds the house,
those who build it labor in vain.

Psalm 127:1

Bless our work, dear Lord,
for all we do is done
in your honor.
Help us to be worthy
to do your work.

Serve the Lord with gladness!
Come into his presence with singing!

Psalm 100:2

When I think of you, Lord,
and all you've done and do,
all the little disappointments
of my day are put in their places
and are quickly forgotten.

*Thy word is a lamp to my feet
and a light to my path.*

Psalm 119:105

Lord, help me to recognize
worthwhile things and study them,
to know your will and do it.

O Lord, our Lord,
  how majestic is thy name
  in all the earth!

                              Psalm 8:9

You've given us
such a beautiful world, Lord...
please show us how to keep it,
and enhance it, and make you glad
that you gave it to us.

The heavens
  are telling the glory of God;
    and the firmament proclaims
    his handiwork.

                    Psalm 19:1

Lord, I am continually reminded
of your power, your strength,
and your majesty
as I look at the earth
and sky around me.

God is our refuge and strength,
a very present help in trouble.

Psalm 46:1

Help me, Lord, to consider
the well-being of others
before thinking of my own
personal comfort.

Great peace have those
who love thy law;
nothing can make them stumble.

Psalm 119:165

Lord, to do your work and your will
is a joy to me and makes me glad
through all my being.

The earth is the Lord's
and the fulness thereof,
the world and those
who dwell therein.

Psalm 24:1

We are in your hands, Lord!
What a wonderful sense
of security and joy
we are able to know because of it!

Let the words of my mouth
and the meditation of my heart
be acceptable in thy sight, O Lord,
my rock and my redeemer.

Psalm 19:14

AMEN.